A Gift To Dance
Cultivating Your Ministry

ShaQuann L. Harris

FOREWORD BY
Bishop Paul S. Morton, Sr.

Copyright © 2018 by ShaQuann L. Harris
All rights reserved. In accordance with the U.S. Copyright Act of 1976, the scanning, uploading, and electronic sharing of any part of this book without the permission of the publisher is unlawful piracy and theft of the author's intellectual property. If you would like to use material from the book, prior written permission must be obtained by contacting the publisher at
info@entegritypublishing.com.

Thank you for your support of the author's rights.

Entegrity Choice Publishing
PO Box 453
Powder Springs, GA 30127
info@entegritypublishing.com
www.entegritypublishing.com
770.727.6517

Designed by Ellie Woznica

Book Cover Photo by Jamyle Phillips Photography
Photography by Jamyle Phillips and Alan Villavasso

Printed in the United States of America

The views expressed in this work are solely those of the authorand do not necessarily reflect the views of the publisher,
and the
publisher hereby disclaims any responsibility for them.

The publisher is not responsible for websites (or their content) that are not owned by the publisher.

Library of Congress Cataloging-in-Publication Data
ISBN 978-1-7325767-0-4
Library of Congress 2018951887

Dedication

God, You are AMAZING! Thank You, God, for keeping me all of these years and never taking Your hand off of me. Thank You for everything. You have brought my way to conquer in my personal life and in ministry. Because of those tests and trials, I am the super dope woman You called me to be!

Thank You for the opportunity to minister to Your people with the gift of Dance. I dedicate everything that I do to You, Father. :)

To all dance ministries across the nation! Continue to strive for excellence and learn to do well (Isaiah 1:17 KJV). Always seek God first in your preparation and ministry moments. I charge you to better yourselves not only as dancers but as leaders, role models, and Kingdom Representatives. I pray that this book helps all starting and even seasoned ministries be better, effective, and knowledgeable of your assignment. Stay humble and keep God first!

Acknowledgments

To my amazing parents, Ernest and Renee, my gratitude for all of their love, support, guidance, and wisdom. My grandmother, Dorothy Clouds, for her love and prayers. My three sisters Kewanda, Dana, and Dawn, for being the best big sisters a girl could ever ask for and being amazing mothers to my niece and nephews, Haley, Tyler, Kierce, and Michael, Jr. To Demarcus, thank you for being a great brother in law and super awesome to me! I love you Dee. Thank you to all of my aunts, uncles, cousins, and my entire family.

To my spiritual parents, Bishop Paul S. Morton, Sr and Co-Pastor Debra B. Morton, for being great messengers of God's word and exemplifying what leading in excellence truly is. Thank you for your spiritual guidance and support!

To my Changing A Generation family for always supporting me and giving encouraging words. Thank you for being receptive to my ministry and allowing it to bless you.

In loving memory of the late Willie Harris, Jr. (1935-1999) and Phalia Harris (1931-2017). My loving grandparents taught me how to serve in ministry as a young girl. I sang in the choir with my Gran-ny and I served as a Junior Usher with the help of my Paw Paw. I miss you both and I pray that my walk with Christ makes you proud!

Contents

Foreword i
Introduction iii
Are You Called Or Are You Bored? 1

Part I: Starting A Dance Ministry
Membership 11
Flexibility 13
Youth & Young Adult Dance Ministries 15
Technique 17
Choreography 21
Leadership Team 23

Part II: Flow
Praise 31
Worship 33
Warfare 35
Travail 37
Celebration 39
Prophetic 41

Part III: Movement
Dance Movement 47
Focus 49
Quality 51
Breakdown 53
Formations 55
Scattered 57
Levels 59

Part IV: Dance Etiquette
Appearance 65
Preparation 67
Garment Care 71
Protect Your Temple 77
Dieting 81

A Message From ShaQuann 83
A Gift To Dance Foundation, Inc. 85
Bibliography 87
Hebrew & Greek Dance Terminology 89
Scripture References 93
About The Author 99
Notes 102

Foreword

I am so proud of ShaQuann. It has been a privilege to watch her flourish and operate in her gift! I have watched her for the past 12 years continuously flow and operate in excellence. I and many others have been blessed by her ministry.

A Gift To Dance is a must read for anyone who desires to develop a dance ministry and enhance their gift and calling. I encourage all starting and seasoned Dance Ministries to buy this book, for it will educate on important techniques and vital information to help you grow and develop your dance ministry. I am confident that this book will help you in so many ways and, most importantly, it will help you understand the ministry of dance.

Bishop Paul S. Morton, Sr.
*Founder, Full Gospel Baptist Church
Fellowship International
Senior Pastor, Changing A Generation Ministries
Atlanta, Georgia
Overseer & Co-Pastor, Greater St. Stephen Ministries,
New Orleans, Louisiana*

Introduction

I'VE ALWAYS BEEN a Dancer—let my mother tell it, I came out of the womb dancing. Growing up in New Orleans we always listened to music in my house. Whether it was Bounce, Gospel, Jazz, R&B, and even Rap, it was blasting through my mother's sound system.

My sister, Kewanda, always played music while cleaning up and helping with my homework. Once the work was done, we danced in the living room. I was eventually enrolled in The Deidre School of Dance; this is where I learned technique, form, and stage presence. This is where my perfectionism was developed. Ms. Deidre did not play— she groomed us into being the best. I can never forget the year our class performance was to Annie's "Its A Hard Knock Life" and "You're Never Fully Dressed Without A Smile." Those were the good days!

My grandparents were heavily involved in ministry at their church, Mars Hill Missionary Baptist Church. It was there I learned how to serve in ministry. I sang in the soprano section with my Granny and I was a Junior Usher. It was always said that I would sing, but my passion was dance. So I never took it seriously; my focus was 5,6,7,8! Soon after my

Paw Paw died, it didn't feel right to be present in that church anymore.

With him being the head deacon, I always looked forward to him leading Devotion. So I stopped attending, and I eventually joined Greater St. Stephen Full Gospel Baptist Church with my mother. From there, I attended church with her, but I did not get involved in ministry there. Coming from a 100 member church to over 5,000 was a bit much for me. I was a faithful pew member.

I danced on every dance team I tried out for in elementary and middle school. In 2005, of course we relocated to Atlanta, GA, due to Hurricane Katrina. I was a Sophomore in high school and totally oblivious to the Atlanta culture—especially when it came to dance. So I didn't join the dance team at Westlake at all. Not because I couldn't master their dance style—I just wasn't feeling it.

Once Greater St. Stephen started a location in Atlanta, we immediately joined. But becoming a pew member was not my mother's cup of tea. She was an Intercessor, so she joined that ministry. I danced but wasn't active. I remember when it was announced that they were holding auditions for the then Karar Dance Ministry, my mother immediately signed me up against my wishes. Our parents see further than us. I just couldn't see myself doing Liturgical Dance. Honestly, I was a twerker at heart—ok?! I couldn't twerk for Jesus! Enough for Him to strike me down for doing the most. But I digress.

I remember standing in a room full of other women and girls in my age group. I was fifteen at the time. Dr. Delainey, the Overseer of Dance for

FGBC, was holding the audition. Her movement was sharp and to the point. I loved it! But me being in my flesh because I didn't feel like being there, I didn't go full out. I could feel the heat com-ing from my mother's eyes. However, in the end, only three were chosen and I was one of them. I was indeed excited yet shocked; I didn't think she would choose me but she saw something in me. Only those who are seasoned in a specific area can see much more than you just starting out.

From there I began rehearsing with the other members, learning what dance ministry was and getting acclimated to the flow of ministry. So far, so good. I grew passionate about it, I took it serious-ly. I couldn't wait to get to rehearsal to prepare for that upcoming Sunday. Two years later it happened: I was dancing with one of my leaders, and the spirit was so heavy this particular Sunday. It was some-thing I had never felt before. Soon I collapsed and I felt God's touch. I felt Him touch me, and I knew it was Him because it was a loving touch and caress on my back. I opened my eyes and no one was there touching me; it was Him. I got the strength to stand and from there I began to minister. I never knew the impact and power that dance had in the church until that Sunday. My life changed that Sunday morning.

I attended different dance conferences and read books on Dance Ministry because it was something I wanted to master and pass on to those who followed me. Twelve years later, I am still in it and committed. A long time ago I tried to stray away, but then God would knock me back in line. He gave me this gift, so therefore I must present it to Him daily. Of course my journey has not been an easy one. I've had a few bumps in the road and made a lot of sacrifices. I've experienced losses with my mother and dealt with hurt and heartbreak. I wanted to stop altogether and just become a pew member all over again. But God kept us and made a way for me to be in place without missing a beat.

Writing this now, I am twenty-seven years old and in the position to share my journey and knowledge with those who will come after me. I am the Co-Director of my dance ministry at my church and the Georgia State Director of Dance for Full Gospel Baptist Church. Preserving and maintaining my passion has helped me along the way. I wrote this book because I see a lot of dance ministries struggling and lack- ing the proper knowledge of their assignment. Most times, they aren't even assigned this task; they're just there just to be seen. Hence, all of the jokes and videos you see making a mockery of us on social media.

On the flip side, there are seasoned dance ministries who aren't being taken seriously because their church doesn't see a need for them. Everything I have learned (and am still learning), I have poured into this book. This isn't just for starting ministries but seasoned ones as well. Study this together and become stronger and united. Your ministry will never be the same!

Are You Called Or Are You Bored?

"The Spirit of the Lord God is upon me; because the Lord hath anointed me to preach good tidings unto the meek; he hath sent me to bind up the brokenhearted, to proclaim liberty to the captives, and the opening of the prison to them that are bound; To proclaim the acceptable year of the Lord, and the day of vengeance of our God; to comfort all that mourn; To appoint unto them that mourn in Zion, to give unto them beauty for ashes, the oil of joy for mourning, the garment of praise for the spirit of heaviness; that they might be called trees of righteousness, the planting of the Lord, that he might be glorified."

Isaiah 61:1-3 (KJV)

Before you begin to plan anything regarding ministry, period, you must determine if you are called to function in this area. Are you called to dance in ministry? Seriously, ask yourself this because this is an important question that requires an honest answer. Did you hear God tell you "Go"? We have plenty of ministries that have developed out of sheer boredom, and they come with all of the bells and whistles.

Garments, makeup, uniformity, technique, and the crowd raves once they're done with their presentation. However, there was no anointing. The dance leader most likely attended one of the best dance schools and has technique for years. Yes, the talent is there, but in the grand scheme of things, where is the oil? Where is the anointing? Your presentation was nice and professional, but all you did was entertain the masses instead of bless them.

The main goal for the dance ministry is to usher in the presence of God to the hearts of man through dance. How can that happen? Well, you first have to be called to do so. Anyone (and I do mean anyone) can get up, put on a beautiful performance, and get a few pats on the back. But those that are called and are fully aware of the assignment can break chains, loose strongholds, and set the atmosphere for change to occur.

Understand that we are not entertainers. We are not the praise team's backup dancers. Ministry is not a show. It is serious business. Being in ministry for over ten years, I've had front row access to plenty of shows and ministry moments. I've experienced those who join just to be seen and show off their technique as well as those who actually have a heart for ministry. The entertaining spirit is one of the main reasons why the dance ministry is never taken seriously.

Have you ever visited a church and noticed that they did not have a dance ministry? Or they did have one, and all they did was look cute during the ministry moment? So, you go up to meet the dance leader (if there is one) and immediately you sense that they're simply not interested in the ministry, period? That, my friend, is what you call bored. Ask yourself are you called? Or are you bored? Were you sitting in the pew one Sunday during praise and worship and realized that a dance ministry would make the experience better because you saw it at another church? Did you take on this responsibility because you wanted something to do to be noticed in the church? If so, you, my dear, are simply bored, and you need to sit yourself down immediately. THERE IS NO ROOM FOR BOREDOM HERE.

Dance is already not fully accepted in the church. Just because a dance ministry is present, does not mean they are accepted. I know plenty of pastors who just entertain the thought of a dance ministry being present in the church, but they do not fully support it. It is often cast aside and not fully involved in the worship experience.

When the dancers are asked to minister, they are either cut short or just cut, period. Totally disregarded for the time they put in to prepare. There's so much prejudice and fear of freedom in the spirit in the church today that many compare ministries to secular when it comes to dance. This is why it is important that you know why you're dancing. To this day, many are still clueless and have lack of understanding in this area. In Jeremiah 31:13-14, it explains how dance will be restored and God's church will be rebuilt:

"Then shall the virgin rejoice in the dance, both young men and old together: for I will turn their mourning into joy, and will comfort them, and make them rejoice from their sorrow. And I will satiate the soul of the priests with fatness, and my people shall be satisfied with my goodness, saith the Lord."

Aren't you amazed to see so many dance ministries appear in churches today? It was prophesied in the Old Testament and very popular during that time. Look at where we are now.

Unfortunately, some churches treat dance as something to keep the young girls busy, and please do not think if you're over eighteen that you can get up there, too! Oh, they would have a fit! Gratefully, not all churches are like that and are actually receptive and appreciate the ministry of dance...but they are still clueless to its importance. That is why it is up to you, the LEADER, to know your place and its importance. As a leader you must meet specific requirements for this assignment:

- You are responsible and accountable for the actions of the ministry.

- Be disciplined, organized, and attentive.
- Share the vision of the church.
- Have a vision for the ministry and be sure to carry out that vision. Make sure that those who follow you carry out that vision as well.
- Prayer is important. Seek God in all areas such as membership, garments, music, how to flow, etc.
- Rules and guidelines must be established for the dancers.
- Interviews and auditions must be held for interested dancers before they can join the ministry. It is out of order to allow dancers to join without a proper introduction to the ministry itself.
- Be likeable and easy to work with. Remember the Minister of Music, Praise Team Leader, and Musical Director are your teammates! You must be on one accord with them at all times; otherwise, it will display chaos during the ministry moments.
- Be faithful and have a heart of service. Working in ministry is only rough when your heart's not in it.
- Be able to choreograph various styles and levels of dance after being led by the Holy Spirit.
- Be skillful in the area of dance and spirit realm. This is why it is important to seek dance training and have a daily devotional time.
- Be strong, be courageous! Never waiver in what God told you to do in regards to the ministry. Stand firm and know that He is in

full control and no man can deter you from adhering to His clear instruction.

- Lead in ALL areas: prayer, worship, Bible Study, fasting, etc. Remember your members are following YOU! Everything that you do they will mimic because you are their leader. Lead them down the right path in these areas; you are accountable for them now.

After a self-analysis, I pray that you KNOW you've been called. You've heard God's voice or felt His touch nudging you into this wonderful world of dance ministry. If so, let's continue!

I
STARTING A DANCE MINISTRY

Everyone gather around and huddle up for this one because this will probably be the most diligent task you will have to complete. Of course, starting anything new won't be easy, especially when the final decision lies in someone else's hands. This is where you put your prayer life to work.

I recommend that you enter into a season of intercession before you present the idea to your Pastor or Minister of Music and really ask God to be in the midst first and foremost. Also, ask that He bless the ministry itself. Make sure that your heart and spirit are aligned with the Word of God and you're in full understanding of its purpose. Often times, the Ministry of Dance is taken as a joke or viewed as entertainment. Both are incorrect ideals. As I previously stated, we are in place "to usher in the hearts of man through dance."

To begin a dance ministry, you must have a passion for giving your gift of dance to the Lord. It is He that gave you the gift of dance. James 1:17 says "Every good and perfect gift is from above, coming down from the Father of the heavenly lights, who does not change like shifting shadows." This is the foundation!

In order to be able to fully give yourself to a ministry or even a commitment, you must have a passion for it. You must know that starting a dance ministry is right for you. You will be able to articulate and teach liturgical dance from your heart.

Once the ministry is accepted, you must make sure that you have the biblical resources on deck.

This is important so that your dancers will have a biblical foundation of dance. You can refer to the Scripture References section of this book, but first let's review what Dance and Liturgical Dance is:

- to move one's body rhythmically, usually to music; to engage in or perform a dance
- to move or seem to move up and down or about in a quick or lively manner

Liturgical Dance is a type of dance movement sometimes incorporated into liturgies or worship services as an expression of worship. Some liturgical dance was common in ancient times or non-western settings, with precedents in the Hebrew religion back to accounts of dancing in the Old Testament.

Membership

ONCE YOU HOLD auditions (which is required and necessary) and select the members, here are some much needed requirements and standards that they must abide by:

- A personal, committed relationship to Jesus Christ
- An attitude of submission and humility to Christ and the leadership of the dance ministry and church
- Support for one another as members
- A Christian walk consistent with the Bible, i.s., a lifestyle of holiness and purity in the way you act, dress, and in the things you do away from, as well as at, church
- Your body, mind, and spirit free from injury and sin in order to be able to minister properly under the power and the anointing of the Holy Spirit
- Daily devotional prayer life, including worship, prayer support for the ministry, the vision of the church, and the harvest of souls
- Appropriate dress as priestly representatives of Jesus Christ at all times
- Faithful attendance of rehearsals, ministry meetings, Bible study, and church services

Flexibility

Patience (There is a season of confirmation and ordination. Trust your leader's wisdom in determining when you are to be released into ministry.)

Remember, being part of a dance ministry is a serious matter for those who want to minister to the Lord in excellence through dance. Always give Him your best for He is a jealous God. He deserves your best at all times!

All potential members should also go into a season of intercession before deciding to join a dance ministry. Your heart and spirit have to be right before taking on the task.

Youth & Young Adult Dance Ministries

I BELIEVE THAT there is a place for everyone in the Kingdom, especially if you're doing His work. As we know, a lot of churches create youth dance ministries to keep the children busy and show them off for holiday programs so that their parents can be proud. The young adults, on the other hand, kind of just blend in with the thirty and up club.

I do believe it is important to have separate dance ministries for these groups. It creates balance for rehearsal purposes and growth not just in dance but in ministry. As a whole, everyone's walk with Christ is different, and each age group will establish its own identity. Regardless of the event, the young adults will not want to go forth with the babies. Let's be realistic here.

Some Young Adult Dance Ministries stem from college students who are away from home and served on a dance ministry at their home church. This gives them the opportunity to continue to flow and still be active in this area. In order to gain membership, you will have to hold auditions per usual and encourage the new recruits to invite those who are also interested to come. The age range normally is 18 – 25; some churches stop at age 35 due to preference. If your church hosts annual days for the Young Adults, this is the perfect time for them to go forth full force.

Same goes for the Youth Dance Ministry. Because they are younger and undeveloped, they will need more time for grooming before they can actually go forth on their own. Start out with the annual youth day first. This will not only prepare them but also expose them to what to expect. Keep in mind that these are children, so they may not learn as quickly as the adults. You must take your time with them and exercise patience. Make it fun as well— this will keep them engaged.

Now, it may sound like I'm putting it like you're babysitting them, but that's not the case at all. Your level of patience and expertise will have to come into play in this area. Or you can have someone in place who is well equipped to teach children. Remember, leaders, you don't have to do it all alone.

Technique

Now that you are establishing a liturgical dance ministry, it is important to begin teaching basic dance techniques. Technique in ballet, modern, or jazz will help prepare your body and the body of your dancers for dance ministry. It will help them connect with their bodies so that they will know how far their body can stretch. Injury prevention is the key. It is the main reason that basic dance technique will help your dance ministry. If you are not technically trained in dance, then taking dance classes as a dance ministry leader will help you pass the knowledge you've gained onto your dance ministry. Having basic dance technique will help you build your choreography as well.

Here are some basic terms:

Plie	A bending of the knees in any of the five positions.
Demi Plie	A half bending of the knees, with heels on the floor.
Grand Plie	A full bending of the knees.

First—Fifth Position

There are five basic positions for the feet in which all steps in classic ballet begin and end, with corresponding positions of the arms. It is assumed that in all these positions the legs are turned out from the pelvis.

- FIRST POSITION: heels touching, feet in a straight line
- SECOND POSITION: feet apart in a straight line
- THIRD POSITION: one foot in front of the other, the heel against the instep
- FOURTH POSITION: feet apart, one in front of the other, either opposite first or opposite fifth
- FIFTH POSITION: one foot in front of the other, the heel against the joint of the big toe

Other Positions

- CHASSE: a sliding step in which one foot "chases" and displaces the other.
- PORT DE BRAS: in ballet, the position of the arms
- POINT: a position on the top of the toes
- ATTITUDE: a pose in which one leg is raised in back or in front with knee bent, usually with one arm raised
- PIQUE: stepping directly onto the point of a foot
- Spotting: a fixing of the eyes on one spot as long as possible during turns to avoid dizziness and to keep one's orientation
- PIROUETTE: a complete turn of the body executed on one leg; the working leg is placed with the foot drawn up to the ankle or knee of the supporting leg.

Dance workshops are very essential because dance evolves every single day. It is important that your ministry is polished at all times. You can flow prophetically but having a little technique will go a long way as well. We can flow and still be in control of the movement. No chaos allowed! It causes a distraction.

Choreography

God does not call us to do something without equipping us for the task. Those who have a call to worship dance will be given the ability to choreograph. This may take time to develop. It is always good to pray first; worship is definitely God's will, so expect Him to answer!

I've found it helpful to play a worship CD and just move freely to this alone at home. You will begin to get some movements to express a few of the words in the song. The movements you get to start with will not be the polished, finished article. You may not get them in chronological order or linking together at the start. If you keep playing the music over and over again, the dance will gradually develop and become more polished. It is also important to pray and worship, asking God to flow through you. The movement will not only come to you but it will be powerful!

Don't be afraid to be creative and expressive with your movement. Be complex, challenging, and intentional with your movement. Each time you go forth, your choreography should be on a higher level than it was the last time.

Leadership Team

As I stated previously, leaders, you do not have to do it all alone. It is important to have a leadership team to assist and pick up where you left off. Also, this provides the opportunity for others to use their gifts.

Overseer/Director

This will be YOU. You are responsible and accountable for the entire dance department. Choreography, dance garment choice, and rehearsal scheduling come from you. You partner with the Minister of Music, Praise Team Leader, and Music Director when planning events and/or just the regular flow for Sunday mornings. All final decisions come from you.

Co-Director(s)

A minimum of two is desirable. This person is the Overseer/Director's right hand. Whenever the Overseer/Director is absent, this person is in charge and must carry out the vision set in place. They are responsible to assist with choreography, meetings, and final decisions dealing with the ministry.

Administrator (Optional)

The Administrator is responsible for making sure that all correspondence regarding rehearsals, garments, events, outings, music, or any changes mandated by the Overseer/Director are sent via email and/or text message to the team. This person is the left hand of the Overseer/Director. This position is optional because most of the time the Overseer and Co-Director(s) handle this role.

Treasurer

The Treasurer is responsible for collecting all dues, payments for garments and/or group outings, fundraising monies, conference registrations, and any other financial obligations delegated by the Overseer/Director.

Young Adult Director

The Young Adult Director represents the Young Adults and leads them in delegated rehearsals. This person is responsible for the choreography for annual days and ministry moments (when scheduled).

Youth Dance Director

The Youth Dance Director is responsible for teaching choreography but also teaching biblical principles, such as Sunday School. The Youth Dance Director must have a heart to work with children and patience.

During the first year of the overall ministry's existence, each chosen leader will have displayed leadership qualities, discipline, commitment, talent, skill, and a walk in God. Of course, everything takes time, so it will be wise to observe and take mental notes. See everyone's potential and then once you make your decision, groom them into great leaders.

> *"Leadership is practiced not so much in words as in attitude and in actions."*
> —Harold S. Greene

II
Flow

IN THIS CHAPTER, you will learn of the different styles of dance and their purpose. It is important to know their meanings as well as the appointed time to flow in them. Remember each dance has a meaning and purpose. Before we dive into that, let's refresh ourselves on the history of dance and its meaning…

According to Merriam-Webster dictionary, "dance" is defined as "to move one's body rhythmically usually to music; to engage in or perform a dance." Although dance is done to music, it is also done non-musically, with natural movement and subconsciously.

Praise

Praise is a covenant. It is not an emotion or need-based movement. We have been ordained to praise by God. Of course, there is biblical evidence: Psalms 146:1-2, Psalms 149:1, 3, and Psalms 150:4, just to name a few. Note, praise is something we do by faith because God has commanded us to do so. It is the entry into the Holy of Holies; it invites us into the presence of God. He inhabits the praises of His people!

Now, I'm sure almost every dance ministry flows during praise and worship at their local church service(s). It's a shocker that a lot of New Age churches don't allow their dancers to go forth during that time, and some don't even have dance ministries at all! (Hence, why this book was written but I digress). During the week, the praise team and band rehearse the songs they will minister at the upcoming service. Dancers, you must be on one accord and know what you are ministering to. It is not only important to be united in dance, but you have to be united with the praise team and musicians. Remember, you are a piece of the puzzle; without you the puzzle is incomplete.

Praise is usually upbeat and repetitive; stamina and excitement are definitely needed. While rehearsing with your ministry, listen to the song given and let it minister to you. From there, movement will come. Also, include your members in the process. Showcase what the Holy Spirit placed inside each of you and create. (Leaders, remember you don't always have to choreograph alone. Include your ministry members as well.) When you go forth, of course the Holy Spirit will have its way and shift the atmosphere. YOU have to be spiritually and physically ready for it. The praise team leader may sing a certain verse repeatedly; you have to flow with them and keep going. Smile, be excited in the Lord. Invite the congregation to clap their hands, jump onto their feet, lift their hands, etc. Praise is an invitation—be inviting while you're ministering.

Worship

From praise we transition into worship (my favorite part of the service). Usually slow and melodic. Worship comes from the heart. It shows devotion and adoration to God. The movement must showcase such. Although we have praised Him and thanked Him for ALL He has done and will do, Worship is loving Him for who He is. Admiring Him in all of His glory. Your movement is a love song to His ears. How to do this you ask? Just think, as we love our spouse, children, material possessions, we showcase that feeling daily with our actions. Do the same for God with your movement in dance.

Worship is just you and God communicating, a personal experience.

Worship is choreographed by the Holy Spirit. During worship, people are healed, delivered, and set free. The anointing flows through the dancers as they dance in the Spirit. When the anointing lifts, be prepared for an experience of different reactions based on how God chooses to express Himself. Chains are broken, ropes are cut loose, and change happens. Often times, worship is treated as a breather because praise just wore you out. Absolutely not! Keep that same passion going. Yes, breathe of course, but keep in mind that YOU may be the only ministry someone in the congregation may receive to bring them to Christ.

Worship is expressive; keep your facial expressions intact during this time. It is inappropriate to keep the same big, exciting smile you had during praise. Transition is key. During worship, your tone is serious and loving; it should show. God may choose to speak prophetically; be open.

Warfare

Warfare is aggressive and filled with sharp movements and sounds such as kicks, punches, feet stomping, marching, yelling, etc. It can include marching around the sanctuary, use of banners and flags, and involving the entire congregation. During warfare, the ministry of pageantry is in full affect. Each flag, streamer, and banner has a meaning and will be fully utilized in this moment.

The dance of warfare is done when a need is made known and can be done by faith to bring deliverance to a congregation, family, city, or country. It can be choreographed or spontaneous. Warfare is used to prepare the atmosphere for the preaching of the Word.

When ministering, there may be a section or person filled with an opposing/demonic spirit. As you offer the sacrifice of praise and go into a warfare praise, that spirit will flee! From there, the people of God will be ready to receive the Word of God.

"Let them praise His name in the dance: let them sing praises unto Him with the timbrel and harp. To execute vengeance upon the heathen, and punishments upon the people; to bind their kings with chains, and their nobles with fetters of iron." Psalms 149:3,7-8 (KJV)

Warfare can be used to get into the anointing. With all of the division and opposition that is now present in the church, we can be change makers and chain breakers as we war in the spirit through dance. Lives will be changed and people will be saved and brought to God. That is the ultimate goal!

We can win and take authority over our homes, family, community, ministry, and government. When you're in warfare, you're in battle. When it is a long battle, the Holy Spirit will lead on a daily basis as needed. Through warfare dance it is a guarantee that our prayers will be answered.

Travail

After we have praised, worshipped, and warred in the Spirit, we begin to travail. Often times travailing and warfare are deemed synonymous. During warfare we are interceding and declaring victory over the principalities of darkness. Travailing is thanking God for answering our prayer before we can even see the end results. Travailing is a dance of faith. It gives birth to His desires and establishes the fulfillment of His purposes in the earth.

Although you can travail through prayer by speaking the Word of God, dancing is less worrisome and more joyful. Expect a great release! As would happen when you are angry or afraid, an adrenaline rush takes place and we gain a second wind. Movement becomes more intense and strong: movements of supplication, power and authority.

It is important for the entire worship department to be on accord in this area, we are all on assignment to dissolve any hindrance that may distract the Pastor while delivering the Word of God. One wrong note or chord can throw the dancers off. Remember, we are all important pieces to the puzzle. During this time, guard your spirit. Often times distractions occur and the assignment is marked incomplete.

Celebration

The dance of celebration can be done in a circle, group, or solo—spontaneous or choreographed. The movements express joy and happiness through jumping, leaping, skipping, twirling, hand clapping, or with an instrument, i.e. tambourine. Often times done in the aisles "Your procession, God, has come into view, the procession of my God and King into the sanctuary. In front are the singers, after them the musicians; with them are the young women playing the timbrels." Psalms 68:24-25 (KJV)

Celebrate simply means to acknowledge, engage in festivities, commemorate, exalt, or cheer. Dance can be used to celebrate a personal or corporate victory, the birth of Jesus Christ, the resurrection of Jesus Christ, etc. Dance was used heavily in the Bible as a sign of celebration. Refer to Deuteronomy 16:1 (Passover), Acts 2:1-4 & Exodus 23:16 (Feast of the Harvest), and Deuteronomy 16:13-15 (Feast of Tabernacles).

The dances that were associated with these events are the torch dance, procession of marching and singing, and children carrying flags and candles. The flags are of the tribe of Judah, which means praise. All dances should be colorful and expressive! Palm branches, candles, torches, streamers, and other ornamental items can be used as props.

Prophetic

THE PROPHETIC DANCE is a dance where the mind of God is expressed so that the congregation not only hears the message from God but also sees the message. It is spontaneous and inspired by the Holy Spirit and can be danced by a single person or group.

Prophetic dance does not have to be danced to singing or any music but may be accompanied by the rhythm of clapping hands, stomping feet, snapping fingers, or done in pure silence. However the Holy Spirit chooses to move is how you flow. It is the dance of warfare, edification, instruction, and foretelling of what's to come.

In order to move prophetically, it has to be done in an orderly fashion. The person or group involved MUST know and understand prophecy. If the persons involved do not normally flow in the prophetic realm outside of ministry, then they will not be able to dance and do prophecy at the same time. Major key: all leaders (meaning the dance leader, praise team leader, music director, and pastor) must be on one accord and learn to flow together; it's the only way the flow will be effective.

Remember, we are not fighting against flesh and blood, but against powers, principalities, rulers of darkness, and wicked spirits in high places (Ephesians 6:12). So it is important that the dance leader have the trust of the pastor; it allows them to flow freely. Be faithful and cooperative with the pastor.

III
Movement

There are different types of movement in dance and each has a place and meaning. It is important that you grasp each movement and know its place. Each movement has an appropriate time and place. Refer to these so you won't be a distraction or cause confusion with your ministry.

Dance Movement

Succession: to create variety or emphasize a point. Dancers may repeat the same movement in succession or, in other words, one after another.

Opposition: to add interest to a dance or to express difference or turmoil. Dancers may move in steps that are in opposition to the other part of the dance ministry.

Unison: all together, alike, as one.

Focus

Focus is another dimension of dance. Direction and point of reference.

- Up: hope, expectation, pride, searching, in need of guidance.
- Away: rejection, denial, shame, no, anger.
- Down: sorrow, humility, inferiority, searching, shame.

Quality

Pendula Movement: a free-swinging movement in the torso, at the knee and elbow. It creates a feeling of openness, naturalness, and freedom.

Sustained Movement: a steady, equalized release of energy with no interruption. Expresses beauty, strength, patience, gracefulness, love, etc.

Percussive Movement: a strong, sharp, aggressive movement. Dodging, throwing, jumping or kicking. Used to express anger, war, rebellion, a troop of soldiers marching, etc.

Vibratory Movement: a quivering or shaking, pulsating movement. Expresses fear, sickness, strength, glory, or sun rays.

Collapse: the absence of any tension, a controlled fall, a complete relaxation of the entire body, or of a particular body part. Expresses being hit, death, exhaustion, giving up, etc.

Breakdown

Jump: to spring, bounce, go over, recoil, to spring upon, pounce, change abruptly, to advance.

Slide: to glide, move smoothly over a surface while keeping continuous contact with the floor.

Leap: to move off the ground with a spring of the legs.

Stag Leap: to leap as a deer by kicking forward with the forward leg and then bending that same leg and stretching the rear leg back to give the move a deep leap appearance.

Contract: to draw together or shrink. Bend the body at the waist and bring chest to knees.

Kick: to strike out with the foot (forward, backward, or sideways).

Turn: to move around a center or axis, also revolve or rotate.

Reach: to stretch out a body part.

Shake/Shiver: to move with short quick movements, to tremble. Expresses fear or being cold.

Formations

Using a variety of formations and floor patterns in dance will add variety and dimension to the dance:
- Line
- Diagonal
- Circle

Scattered

Each formation can be used in various combinations and can adequately express an idea as they combine with proper dance movements.

Levels

When dancing before the Lord, the movements used and the levels used in the dance have a certain meaning. Here are a few examples:

- Lying down: to surrender to God, in awe of God, to show death, sleeping, exhaustion, defeat, total submission.
- Kneeling: prayerfulness, begging, repentance, worship, humility, etc.
- Sitting: rest, sitting at someone's feet, pondering, giving up, etc.
- Standing: praise, confidence, strength, victory, etc.
- Jumping: rejoicing, victory, frustration, force, warfare, etc.

IV
Dance Etiquette

THIS IS THE meat and potatoes of this book. Etiquette is very important in Dance. Just like if you were an Elder or Senior Pastor of a church, you are required to conduct yourself accordingly as a Minister of Dance. Since we are the most ridiculed ministry in the church (in my opinion), it's smart not to add fuel to the fire. We are still leaders. So therefore, we must act accordingly. How we carry ourselves in and out of the house sets the tone on how we will be received.

Unfortunately, people in the church are very fickle. I'm not saying you have to wear the purest of pure garments every time you step out but make sure your attire is appropriate. Especially if you're the leader of that ministry. In this case, I will address those who are reading as leaders.

Appearance

Once again, your appearance has to be up to par, not just in the pulpit but in the congregation as well. Your garments should not only reflect holiness but also, responsibility. We must not go forth and our garments are dirty, stained with last week's makeup, or wrinkled. Every dance ministry should have an iron/steamer and static guard on hand in the dressing room. For upkeep it is best to send your garments to the dry cleaners at the end of each month; it will keep them fresh, pressed, and free of discoloration.

Now, if you are on a budget, you can always wash your garments in cold water and hang to dry. This avoids shrinkage and discoloration; just make sure that you have a steamer on deck to keep them wrinkle-free. Your garments are priestly, so treat them as such.

As you enter the church, carry them in a hanging garment bag. Never come to church dressed in your garments. Always arrive in appropriate dancewear, covering your "blessed parts."

It is important to arrive at least one hour before it is time to minister so you can get ready and consecrate as a group. Do a dress check to prevent any malfunctions and distractions once you go forth. Please make sure that you have safety pins, band aids, wipes, bobby pins, and deodorant in reach for these are lifesavers!

Makeup is optional. If you decide that you want your face beat for God literally, please do so in decency and in order. No loud colors—it's distracting. Light browns and other earthly tones are acceptable. Pinks and nudes are desirable for lipstick and/or lip gloss. Please make sure that your foundation does not bleed, for you will be sweating during worship.

Keep your hair out of your face, for it can be distracting to you and the congregation. Desirable hair styles include: low buns, ponytails, or if you have long hair pin, it behind your ears and out of your face. Headbands must match your garment for uniformity purposes.

Studs and pearls are the appropriate earrings for ministry moments, period. No hoops or chandelier earrings are allowed. They can cause injury if your garment or flag gets hooked to it. We want to make sure you are not causing a hazard to yourself. If you are not comfortable with wearing earrings while ministering, it is appropriate to not wear them. Please ensure that anything that you may wear while ministering does not cause a hindrance to you or the Spirit. Use logic.

Preparation

Pray. Pray. Pray! Your prayer life will increase when you're in a dance ministry, especially as the leader. It is important that you keep the ministry and yourself covered by the Blood of Jesus and seek His guidance in everything that you do concerning the ministry and your personal life. Pray that His anointing flows as you all minister; it is needed.

Father God, I come to You with thanksgiving and praise. Thank You for the opportunity to thank You once more, Oh God. Thank You for being just who You are and all that You are to me. You are the love of my soul, the reason I dance for Your glory each and everyday, dear Lord. I thank you for choosing me to be a willing vessel to do Your works through Dance. I ask that You cover me from the crown of my head to the soles of my feet. Let your anointing flow through me, God. Continue to let Your oil burn within me. Holy Spirit, have Your way in this place today. I invite Your presence in as I minister to Your people. Purify my heart and spirit, Father, so that Your spirit may spill out onto Your people. Let someone, even if it is just one, be blessed and come to You to today. I know my assignment and, with your strength, it shall be completed. Let us all be on one accord so the atmosphere can be set to receive

Your word from the Man of God. I bind any injuries, nervousness, and distractions right now in the name of Jesus. We claim the victory now and thank You in Jesus' name. Amen!

Pray as you choreograph for the upcoming ministry moment; the movement will come to you more clearly and release the frustration of trying to get it right off of you. As a choreographer, I often times get into a place of frustration because I am a perfectionist, and it has be powerful. So, I seek God in this area and just let Him have His way. Because at the end of the day, it's not about me! Or how well I can dance. It's about His glory being televised through my movement. Remember that.

Everyone on schedule to go forth that upcoming Sunday or included in the special piece that will be ministered is mandated to be at ALL rehearsals, especially the final rehearsal. If it is not communicated to the powers that be of any arising conflicts or absences, then it is appropriate for this person to sit out. Reason being, everyone must be on one accord and have the choreography conditioned in their spirit before going forth. Stay prepared so you won't have to prepare. By doing so, attending rehearsals is key.

Also, remember to stretch daily. This keeps your body limber and able to endure certain movement without strain on your muscles. Be sure to warm up before you do any physical movements. Stay hydrated! I can't begin to tell you how many times I have seen dancers fall out due to dehydration. Yes, the Lord is our strength and we can do all things through Him...but He also gave us wisdom! Use it and drink some water please!

PREPARATION

"For the Lord gives wisdom; from his mouth come knowledge and understanding."
—Proverbs 2:6 (NIV)

Garment Care

I know I touched on garment care in the previous section, but let's talk about their importance and meaning, shall we? From there, you will understand the urgency of taking care of them. When purchasing new garments, the first thing to consider is the color and overall fit. You will have some members who are blessed and highly favored; however, this does not need to be magnified during the ministry moments.

Be mindful not to choose a garment just because it's pretty or fitting. Yes, the garment must be appealing to the eye, but it has to be flowy and somewhat loose (just a little). For the members who are highly favored, they will be required to purchase an overlay if the garment is somewhat tight-fitting up top. Jumping and praising Him will cause some jiggling... you get what I'm saying. No distractions allowed!

How does a garment have meaning and how does it represent the song we're ministering to? Simply put: the colors. Did you know that each color has a meaning? Check this out:

- WHITE: Purity, Holiness, Cleansing of Sin, Peace, Light
- PINK/ROSE: Rose of Sharon, Tenderness, Innocence

- Red: Blood of Jesus, Redemption, Warfare, Salvation
- Green: Freedom, Renewal, New Beginning, Hope
- Blue/Turquoise: The Living Water, Spirit of God, Heaven, Hope, Healing, Holy Spirit
- Purple: Royalty, The Throne of God, Majesty, Noble, Heir, Kingship, Authority
- Orange: Fire of God, Flames, Harvest, Spiritual Warfare
- Gold: Glory of God, Divinity, Refinement
- Iridescent: Overcoming
- Rainbow: Covenant, God's Promises
- Black: Eternity, Constancy, Darkness, Sin, Judgment, Death
- Grey/Silver: Redemption, Word of God, Purity, Righteousness
- Yellow: Joy, Celebration, Light, Happiness

"Study and shew thyself approved unto God, a workman that needeth not to be ashamed, rightly dividing the word of truth."

—2 Timothy 2:15 (KJV)

This list is the key to choosing your garments effectively and not because they look pretty. Each garment shall have a message behind them as well as the song you minister to. Everything should be cohesive from garments to movement. Each dress should be accompanied with a matching pair of palazzo pants. It's amazing to me how some dance ministries don't wear palazzo pants underneath their dresses. Shocking! Your tops should be loose fitting and cover your blessed parts, along with a skirt and/or palazzo pants.

For the men, you are required to wear tops that cover you as well as the appropriate undergarments to hold you in place. I've noticed that when you're not properly covered, you cause a distraction. Keep our eyes to hills and not the valley!

David and the high priests wore tunics, robes, sashes, ephods, headbands, a breast piece, and undergarments each skillfully crafted. In Exodus 28 and 29 it perfectly describes the garments and their purpose:

ROBE—It was entirely blue with an opening for the head in its center. It had a woven edge like a collar around the opening so that it did not tear. The hem was trimmed in blue, purple, and scarlet yarn with gold bells between them. The sound of the bells was heard as Aaron entered into the Holy Place before the Lord and when he came out. This allowed him not to die because only the high priests could enter into the Holy Place.

EPHOD – This is the most important item of the priestly garments, similar to an apron and made of materials woven out of gold and linen thread. It was made of gold, blue, purple, and scarlet yarn and twisted linen. It covers the back and chest and reaches to the knees. It fastens to the body by two straps and a wristband. Also, two shoulder pieces are attached to two of its corners for fastening.

THE BREAST PIECE – Similar to the ephod, it was made in gold, blue, purple, and scarlet yarn and twisted linen. It was made square, a span long, a span wide, and folded double. It had four rows of precious stones mounted on it. It had two braided gold rings for it to fasten at the two corners of the breast piece. Two more gold rings were attached to the other two corners of it on the inside and two more rings attached at the bottom of the shoulder pieces on the front of the ephod. As a memorial to the Lord, the names of the sons of Israel were engraved over the heart. This was Aaron's breast piece that he wore every time he entered into the Holy Place.

Tunics/Sashes/Headbands/Undergarments — A blue cord was fastened to the front of the turban. It was worn on Aaron's forehead as a reminder of the guilt involved in the sacred gifts the Israelites had consecrated so they would be acceptable to the Lord. These garments represented dignity and honor and were made with the finest linen. The undergarments hold everything in place underneath the overall garment itself. Undergarments include: unitard, leotard and leggings, spanx (if needed), and tights. Wearing undergarments is a requirement!

> *"I delight greatly in the Lord; my soul rejoices in my God. For he has clothed me with garments of salvation and arrayed me in a robe of his righteousness, as a bridegroom adorns his head like a priest, and as a bride adorns herself with her jewels."*
> —Isaiah 61:10 NIV

Keeping up with your garments, as we touched on in the previous section. should be top priority. We cannot present our gifts back to God dirty and wrinkled. Abide by the following:

- Have your pastor consecrate your new garments.

- Keep your garments hanging up at all times. Do not throw them on the floor.
- Iron or steam them to keep wrinkles out. Also keep static guard in your dance bag or ministry dressing room.
- Store in a hanging garment bag. Never fold and place inside duffle bag.
- Keep them clean! Send your garments at the end of each month to the dry cleaners. Another alternative is to wash in cold water and hang dry. This will eliminate shrinkage and discoloration.

Protect Your Temple

I CANNOT EXPRESS this enough, but it is imperative to take care of ourselves. It makes no sense to me when I visit other churches and their dancers are out of shape and out of breath by the second verse! Now I am not saying that you have to have a build like Beyoncé or Dwayne Johnson, but be healthy and conditioned to go forth without any complications. You can't give your all to God tired and short of breath.

Leaders, I charge you to promote a light diet and workout regimen to your members. No, you do not have to go vegan or work out twenty times a week, but condition your body to be able to handle the warfare. Spirit warfare is not just spirit; it's mental and physical as well. I want you to be strong in all of those areas, for your assignment requires as such.

In rehearsal, before you go over any type of choreography, you should warm up and stretch. Warm up first to prevent any muscle sprains during the stretch. Push, but not too hard; this is an injury free zone! Encourage your members to stretch and push themselves to be better and more flexible. Coordination, agility, flexibility, and stamina are important in dance. During your warm up, the key areas you should warm are the neck, shoulders, back, arms, legs, and hips. Also, treat your feet doing point and flex exercises.

- **NECK ROTATIONS** – slowly roll your head to the right
- **SHOULDER ROLLS** – roll your shoulders forward 8-10 times and then repeat backwards
- **BACK STRETCH** – slowly lift your arms above your head and roll forward, keeping your arms straight and parallel with your hips. You should be in a flat position. Slowly lift your head and rotate left to right while extending your arms further.
- **ARM ROTATIONS** – stretch your arms out horizontally and make a fist. Proceed to roll your arms forward 8-10 times and then repeat backwards
- **LEG LIFTS** – place hands on hips or stretch out horizontally for balance. Lift right leg forward, pointing the toe, for an 8 count then slowly lower the leg for an 8 count.
- **HIP SWITCH** — Lying on your back with your legs straight on the ground, extend your arms out to your sides so your body forms a T. Lift your right leg straight up in the air over your body, hinging at the hip, and drop the entire leg across your body, touching the ground with your right foot to the left of your body. Lift the leg back up, return it to the original position, and repeat with the left leg. You should feel your lower back and hips twisting with each of these motions.

This will help warm and loosen up your muscles before starting exercise and learning choreography.

I cannot stress enough how important it is to be safe and prevent injury. Everyone's limits are not the same; it is your duty to make sure that they push to get there without hurting themselves.

Dieting

Aside from proper exercise habits, dieting is a major component as well. Encourage your members to eat healthy and have an exercise regimen to keep their stamina up. Having a healthy lifestyle is an important aspect of being a dancer.

Proper fuel for the dancer's body is extremely important in order to maintain proper energy levels, avoid injury, and for overall appearance. In order to be successful in this area, exercise together— nothing too strenuous but enough to build up the heart rate. It takes a lot more than a wing and a prayer; you have to use wisdom and take care of yourself.

Always stay hydrated, drink plenty water and/or Gatorade before and after ministering. Because you sweat during warfare, it's essential that you put back what you put out. Drink up! Have healthy snacks such as nuts, trail mix, fruit, and granola bars available; going hard for the Lord can make you hungry sometimes! Include in your diet the proper proteins, fats, carbohydrates, vitamins, and minerals.

Protein: This is an important component with regard to maintaining, producing, and repairing essential lean muscles in the body. Without adequate protein levels to fuel muscles, your body would not have the strength to minister at such great levels that are required. Great protein infused foods are poultry, beans, tofu, legumes, and certain types of fish.

FATS: I know we all love fried chicken, but that isn't the type of fats we're looking to include in the diet. There are good fats, you know. Those include avocados, nuts, fish, and seafood. There are plenty of meals you can create with these good fats. Be creative!

CARBOHYDRATES: When you think of carbohydrates, you think starch, which can be fattening. However, that is not fully the case here. Carbohydrates should comprise a majority of your diet. Reason being, carbs stay in your system much longer than sugar. So no Snickers for you! Having a high carb diet will hinder the food from moving through you so quickly and actually staying in your system. This allows it to continue to feed your body and produce more energy. Trust me, you're going to need it. Some great carbs are bagels, brown rice, cereals, breads, potatoes, and pastas. Yummy!

VITAMINS AND MINERALS: I highly advise that you invest in a bottle of One A Day Multivitamins. They are available for men and women. It has all of the essential vitamins you need to intake in just one pill. You literally take "one a day," pretty cool, right? Now these are responsible for the red blood cell formation and maintenance as well as sufficient energy production. In addition, certain vitamins support bone health and formation which is essential for dancers. So in addition to eating the proper foods and exercising daily, the proper intake of vitamins will also help you go a very long way. You will thank me later. :)

A Message From ShaQuann

Hey, Ministers of Dance,

I pray that everything you have read in this book will help you cultivate your ministry to the level it should be. I have given as much information as I could so that you can be successful and have a better understanding in this area. It is my desire that you understand the purpose of your call and assignment.

Dance Ministry is no joke! It requires sacrifice, intention, and hard work...did I mention sacrifice? Yes, be prepared for that, but I promise it is so worth it because in the end God will be glorified. It is my passion to teach and help others in this area. I understand that many require hands-on training, which is great because I will be hosting and teaching at my conference, A Gift To Dance every September in Atlanta, GA. Also, for more hands-on training, I will be having a retreat for Dance Ministry Leaders every March. I not only want to help you develop into a successful Dance Ministry but also fellowship and unite. It amazes me how so divided we are... so let's change that!

By the time you have read this, I pray that I have ministered with you or at least shaken your hand. Remember - stay humble, prayed up, and focused on Him!

Be Blessed,
ShaQuann L. Harris
Author

A Gift To Dance Foundation, Inc.

A Gift To Dance Foundation, Inc. is a non-profit that specializes in dance and technique training for children with autism. Our method of teaching includes providing a calm, intimate environment where they will feel comfortable and wanted. This helps boost their stamina and confidence and enhances their social skills. We train to Gospel, Jazz, and Hip Hop music, for these help uplift their spirits and place them in the atmosphere of worship, spiritual refuge, and high energy. Our headquarters are located in Atlanta, GA.

A Gift To Dance was founded by myself, ShaQuann L. Harris, because I had a passion for teaching children and wanted to give back to my community.

Please visit www.agifttodance.org for more information, upcoming events, and donation opportunities.

BIBLIOGRAPHY

Kovacs, A. (2011). Dancing into the Anointing: Touching the Heart of God Through Dance. Shippensburg, PA: Destiny Image.

Nelson, T. (1997, 1999). The New Strong's Concise Concordance and Vine's Concise Dictionary of the Bible. Two Bible Reference. Classics in One Handy Volume. Nashville: Thomas Nelson, Inc.

Strong, J, LL.D., S.T.D. (2001). The Strongest Strong's Exhaustive Concordance of the Bible. 21st Century Edition. Grand Rapids: Zondervan.

Hedgeman, D. (2007). Guidelines to Starting and Maintaining a Church Dance Ministry. Tate Pub. & Enterprises.

Scofield, C. I., and Henry G. Weston. (1996)The Scofield Study Bible: the Holy Bible, Containing the Old and New Testaments, Authorized King James Version: with a New System of Connected Topical References to All the Greater Themes of Scripture, with Annotations, Revised Marginal Renderings, Summaries, Definitions, Chronology, and Index, to Which Are Added, Helps at Hard Places, Explanations of Seeming Discrepancies, and a New System of Paragraphs. Oxford University Press.

Webster. (Ed.). (1982). Dance. Retrieved March 03, 2018, from https://www.merriam-webster.com/dictionary/dance?utm_campaign=sd

Unknown. (2016). Significance of Praise Dance Garment Colors. Retrieved July 03, 2018, from http://trulyanointedscarves.com/Significance_Praise_Dance_Garment_Colors.html

Unknown. (2016). Dance Terms, Definitions, Terminology. Retrieved December 03, 2017, from https://www.centralhome.com/ballroom-country/dance_terms.htm

Unknown. (2001). Healthy diet for dancers & daily routine:. Retrieved December 03, 2017, from http://www.dance-america.com/healthy-diet-for-dancers-30.html

HEBREW & GREEK DANCE TERMINOLOGY

1. Chiwl (Khool) - to twist or whirl in circular motion or spiral manner. To travail in pain or fear.
   a) Judges 21:21
   b) Psalms 96:9
2. Chagag (Kwaw - gag) to move in a circle; to march in a sacred procession; to observe a festival.
   a) Exodus 12:14
   b) Leviticus 23:41
   c) Deuteronomy 16:15
3. Mechowlah (Mekh-o-law) - a dance; company; dances
   a) Exodus 15:20
   b) Judges 21:21
   c) 1 Samuel 21:11
   d) Song of Solomon 6:13
4. Haliykah (Hal-ee-kaw) - a walking caravan; procession; march
   a) Psalms 68:24-25
5. Halal (Haw-lal) - to shine; boast; brag; foolish; to rave
   a) 1 Chronicles 16:4
   b) Ezra 3:10, 11
   c) Psalms 145:3,9
6. Machowl (Maw-khole) - a round dance
   a) Psalms 30:11
   b) Jeremiah 31:4
   c) Lamentations 5:15

7. Towdah (To-dah) - to extend the hands; adoration; a choir of worshippers; sacrifice
   a) Nehemiah 12:31, 38, 40
   b) Psalms 50:14
   c) Jeremiah 33:11
8. Giyl (Gheel) - to spin around under the influence of any violent emotion
   a) Psalms 2:11
   b) Psalms 31:7
   c) Psalms 35:9
   d) Psalms 43:4
   e) Joel 1:16
   f) Proverbs 2:14
9. Yadah (Yaw-dah) - to worship with extended hands
   a) Psalms 63:4
   b) Psalms 107:8
   c) 1 Chronicles 16:4
   d) 1 Kings 8:33
10. Karar (Kaw-rar) - to dance
    a) 2 Samuel 6:14
    b) 2 Samuel 6:16
11. Raqad (Raw-kad) - to stomp; to spring about wildly; to jump, leap or skip
    a) 1 Chronicles 15:29
    b) Job 21:11
    c) Psalms 29:6
    d) Psalms 114:4, 6

12. Dalag (Daw-lag) - to spring or leap
    a) 2 Samuel 22:30
    b) Psalms 18:29
    c) Song of Solomon 2:8
    d) Isaiah 35:6
    e) Zephaniah 1:9
13. Alaz (Aw-laz) - to jump for joy triumphantly
    a) Psalms 28:7
14. Pazaz (Paw-zaz) - a strong leap or spring
    a) Genesis 49:24
    b) 2 Samuel 6:16
    c) 1 Kings 10:18
15. Qaphats (Kaw-fats) - to draw together close; to leap by contracting the limbs; skips
    a) Song of Solomon 2:8
16. Shiyr (Sheer) - to sing or the idea of strolling minstrelsy
    a) Exodus 15:21
    b) 1 Chronicles 15:27
    c) Psalms 137:3
    d) Jeremiah 20:13
17. Agalliao (Ag-al-lee-ah) - welcome; gladness; exceeding joy
    a) Luke 1:14
    b) Luke 1:44

18. Hallomai (Hal-lom-ahee) -to jump, gush, leap or spring up
    a) John 4:14
    b) Acts 14:10
19. Exallomai (Ex-al-lom-ahee) - to leap
    a) Acts 3:8
20. Skirtao (Skeer-tah-o) - to jump; sympathetically move
    a) Luke 1:41
    b) Luke 1:44
    c) Luke 6:23
21. Orcheomai (Or-kheh-om-ahee) - to dance in a row or ring
    a) Matthew 11:17
    b) Matthew 14:6
    c) Mark 6:22
    d) Luke 7:32
22. Choros (Khor-os) - round dance
    a) Luke 15:25
23. Prochoros (Prokh-or-os) - deacon of the early church; leader of the dance
    a) Acts 6:5
24. Choregeo (Khor-ayg-eh-o) - to be a dance leader; give; minister
    a) 2 Corinthians 9:10
    b) 1 Peter 4:11

Scripture References

Foundation

Isaiah 1:17 - "Learn to do well; seek judgment, relieve the oppressed, judge the fatherless, plead for the widow."

Isaiah 61: 1-3 - "The Spirit of the Lord God is upon me; because the Lord hath anointed me to preach good tidings unto the meek; he hath sent me to bind up the brokenhearted, to proclaim liberty to the captives, and the opening of the prison to them that are bound; To proclaim the acceptable year of the Lord, and the day of vengeance of our God; to comfort all that mourn; To appoint unto them that mourn in Zion, to give unto them beauty for ashes, the oil of joy for mourning, the garment of praise for the spirit of heaviness; that they might be called trees of righteousness, the planting of the Lord, that he might be glorified."

Jeremiah 31:13-14 - "Then shall the virgin rejoice in the dance, both young men and old together: for I will turn their mourning into joy, and will comfort them, and make them rejoice from their sorrow. And I will satiate the soul of the priests with fatness, and my people shall be satisfied with my goodness, saith the Lord."

James 1:7 - "For let not that man think that he shall receive any thing of the Lord."

Ephesians 6:12 - "For we wrestle not against flesh and blood, but against principalities, against powers, against the rulers of the darkness of this world, against spiritual wickedness in high places."

Substance of Movement

Psalms 146:1-2 - *"Praise ye the Lord. Praise the Lord, O my soul. While I live will I praise the Lord: I will sing praises unto my God while I have any being."*

Psalms 149:1 & 3 - *"Praise ye the Lord. Praise the Lord, O my soul. Put not your trust in princes, nor in the son of man, in whom there is no help."*

Psalms 68:24-25 - *"They have seen thy goings, O God; even the goings of my God, my King, in the sanctuary. The singers went before, the players on instruments followed after; among them were the damsels playing with timbrels."*

Psalms 150:4 - *"Praise him with the timbrel and dance: praise him with stringed instrumentsand organs."*

Psalms 149:3, 7-8 - *"Let them praise his name in the dance: let them sing praises unto him with the timbrel and harp. To execute vengeance upon the heathen, and punishments upon the people; To bind their kings with chains, and their nobles with fetters of iron."*

Festivals

Deuteronomy 16:1 - *"Observe the month of Abib, and keep the passover unto the Lord thy God: for in the month of Abib the Lord thy God brought thee forth out of Egypt by night."*

Deuteronomy 16:13-15 - *"Thou shalt observe the feast of tabernacles seven days, after that thou hast gathered in thy corn and thy wine: And thou shalt rejoice in thy feast, thou, and thy son, and thy daughter, and thy manservant, and thy maidservant, and the Levite, the stranger, and the fatherless, and the widow, that are within thy gates. Seven days shalt thou keep a solemn feast unto the Lord thy God in the place which the Lord shall choose: because the Lord thy God shall bless thee in all thine increase, and in all the works of thine hands, therefore thou shalt surely rejoice."*

Acts 2:1-4 - *"And when the day of Pentecost was fully come, they were all with one accord in one place. And suddenly there came a sound from heaven as of a rushing mighty wind, and it filled all the house where they were sitting. And there appeared unto them cloven tongues like as of fire, and it sat upon each of them. And they were all filled with the Holy Ghost, and began to speak with other tongues, as the Spirit gave them utterance."*

Exodus 23:16 - *"And the feast of harvest, the firstfruits of thy labours, which thou hast sown in the field: and the feast of ingathering, which is in the end of the year, when thou hast gathered in thy labours out of the field."*

Preparation

Proverbs 2:6 - *"For the Lord giveth wisdom: out of his mouth cometh knowledge and understanding."*

2 Timothy 2:15 - *"Study to shew thyself approved unto God, a workman that needeth not to be ashamed, rightly dividing the word of truth."*

Isaiah 61:10 - *"I will greatly rejoice in the Lord, my soul shall be joyful in my God; for he hath clothed me with the garments of salvation, he hath covered me with the robe of righteousness, as a bridegroom decketh himself with ornaments, and as a bride adorneth herself with her jewels."*

About The Author

ShaQuann was born and raised in New Orleans, LA. She began dancing at the age of four at The Deidre School of Dance. From there, her passion for dance was ignited. She participated in several recitals and performed on different dance teams.

In August 2005, she and her mother transitioned to Atlanta, GA, due to Hurricane Katrina. She later joined Changing A Generation FGBC (then Greater St. Stephens FGBC) and joined the Karar Dance Ministry (then) at the age of 15. She was the youngest of the founding members of the dance ministry.

Taking full responsibility for the gift and calling God placed on her life, she took the ministry of dance seriously. She has been afforded the opportunity to dance in several productions, choreograph numerous pieces and presentations, and minister on live television.

She is skilled and trained in liturgical, contemporary, jazz, modern, and African dance. She also has 6 years of dance instruction, teaching young girls ages 12 to 17 for after-school programs in East Point, College Park, and Atlanta, GA.

ShaQuann serves as the Director of Dance in Georgia for the Full Gospel Baptist Church Fellowship International and Co-Director of Anointed Vessels Of Worship Dance Ministry at Changing A Generation Full Gospel Baptist Church under the leadership of Bishop Paul S. Morton, Sr. and Dr. Debra B. Morton in Atlanta, GA.

She is currently furthering her studies at Emory University for Business Administration and Dance and Movement Studies. ShaQuann is the Founder and Conference Host of A Gift To Dance Conference. She is also the Founder of A Gift To Dance Foundation, Inc. which specializes in teaching technique and movement classes to children with autism.

NOTES

NOTES

P.O. Box 453
Powder Springs, Georgia 30127

www.entegritypublishing.com
info@entegritypublishing.com
770.727.6517

www.ingramcontent.com/pod-product-compliance
Lightning Source LLC
Chambersburg PA
CBHW052058070526
44584CB00017B/2243